12 Ways You Can Tell at a Glance . . .
Is This the Right Book for You?

If you have ever been in love . . .

If you have ever hoped that love is not in vain . . .

If you have ever wondered what on earth is love all about . . .

If you have ever asked yourself, "Is love really worth the cost?" . . .

If you have ever realized that you don't know how to love . . .

If you have ever thought to yourself that love would consume you . . .

If you have ever been moved by the idea that God is love . . .

If you have ever been hurt by love . . .

If you have ever given up something you love for the sake of love . . .

If you have ever prayed for a Higher form of love . . .

If you have ever had your love rejected . . .

If you have ever sensed a Love awaits you beyond your ability to imagine . . .

Then . . . You may rest assured: *This book is for you.*

"All loves should simply be stepping stones to the love of God. So it was with me; and blessed be his name for his great goodness and mercy."

~ PLATO

APPRENTICE
OF THE
HEART

APPRENTICE
OF THE
HEART

*Lessons in Life
Only Love Can Teach*

GUY FINLEY

WHITE CLOUD PRESS
Ashland, Oregon

Inquiries should be addressed to:
White Cloud Press, PO Box 3400, Ashland, Oregon 97520.
Website: www.whitecloudpress.com

First printing: 2004

Cover photograph by Eric Alan
Cover design by David Ruppe

Printed in the United States of America

Library of Congress Cataloging-in-Publication Data

Finley, Guy.
Apprentice of the heart : lessons in life only love can teach / by
Guy Finley.
p. cm.
ISBN 1-883991-58-7 (pbk.)
1. Love. I. Title: Lessons in life only love can teach. II. Title.
BF575.L8F524 2004
152.4'1--dc22
2003025141

Table of Contents

In deep appreciation to my beloved wife Patricia
for all of her loving help with this Work . . .

This book is dedicated to those
For whom the Good is all things.

What This Book Is About
In Less Than A Few Heartbeats

Seated in the center of the heart, as surely as the essence of a tiny seed holds the promise of a towering tree, lives within us the Presence of a Power that can dispel any gathering darkness and change what is unkind into conscious compassion. What is this great Presence and Power lying latent within us? *It is Love.*

No matter who we are, all of us have known some kind of love in our lives. Love has as many forms on this earth as there are human hearts to reflect and reveal her countless expressions. There is the love we may feel for objects and places, the love we know through relationships with those closest to us, and there is the love of excellence, of natural beauty, and of all things shining bright with unfulfilled promise.

But as stirring, fine, and noble as these loves may be, they tell but a small part of a much greater story hidden from plain sight, yet evident to those with "eyes to see"; for just as radiant energy from the sun, which is not the sun itself, reaches down into creation to animate all of its myriad forms, so is it true that behind and above the everyday loves we have known there dwells an abiding Love of a far greater magnitude; an unseen and supernal Love whose emanations make all other loves possible.

It is this higher, Divine Love that teaches us about love in all its forms, initiating us into the mysteries of our own heart by gently wiping away the borders that stand between our love and our beloved, so that two become as one. Beethoven, Rembrandt, Curie, and Einstein — these and other great souls didn't so much master their respective arts, as much as a great love for their art served to master them. Love educates whoever will embrace her. So it can be for us; to become masters of our own lives we need only learn how to let Love master us.

Apprentice of the Heart is a seven-year chronicle — the story of a beautiful and mysterious dialogue between the author and his Beloved — Divine Love "herself", who — as he reports, "stole into his heart and then ran away with it."

In very personal tones this book touches upon dozens of delicate lessons that are part of our preparation for Love; through them we are helped to realize a timeless Love without whose relationship we cannot hope to know the inner wholeness that is happiness itself. But what are these lessons?

Each heartache, every disappointment, all crowning moments by which we win or lose the object of our desire — that at the time seem the very summit or valley of our lives — each such moment is but one small step along the path that Love has prepared for us to learn her Ways. And that all of us share in these kind of everyday experiences — whose touch deftly transforms our collective heart — proves the point: the Divine Love of which we speak is not meant only for elected sages and hallowed saints. If this were true, then we would have nothing within us to recognize the glow of that small ember in our hearts toward whose warmth and faint light we are drawn. So be assured that where there is an ember, there can also be a flame.

And that by the light of such a fire burning in each of our hearts, if we so will it, our world can be as the Divine intended it to be: a realm of reality that has realized the promise and the fulfill-ment of Love itself.

~ GUY FINLEY

Introduction

Whenever we love someone (even a natural wonder or common creature), we know that our own higher emotional state awakens in us a kind of exalted energy; one that seems to melt barriers and that brings us into relationship with our beloved in ways beyond our understanding. But that's not all: not only does this unseen force of life grant us access to the secret regions of our beloved's heart but, in some mysterious way, it also forges a union between what were formerly separate beings; two become as one for as long as this permeating presence prevails. What do these insights teach us?

In many ways yet to be discovered, Love is the invisible "Third Party" that makes it possible for any two people to be in love; she is the invisible common ground that allows them to be united in a *"place and time"* that neither may know without the other. Love is the catalyst of their completion within one another, even as she is the one Heart being shared between them. And if all this sounds a bit mysterious, that's because Love *is* a Grand Mystery . . . which brings us to what this book is about: how Love works endlessly in Her own secret ways to conquer the willing heart; and how each and every one of us — realized or not — is an apprentice of the Heart, being prepared by Love for Love. Let's look to see if our own past experiences with love won't help us to prove this last important idea.

When we first fall in love with someone we hang on to every word he or she speaks. We don't miss a thing. We notice how they say what is said, the way they move and to what they are drawn; we note all the little things that please them, or that don't. *Nothing* escapes our attention. What is this great desire of ours that so drives us to want to delight the one we love? What the eye can't see, the heart alone perceives:

> *According to our wish and willingness to give our love to another, there returns to us* — in greater measure than given — *the love we have given.* It is, quite simply, the secret of the ages: *Love rewards the lover.*

Isn't it true? The more we love someone, *the more love we come upon in our own being*; and the more we experience these elevated states in ourselves, the higher we long to go! But as we all know, visiting such heavens has proven itself perilous; for even while we hope that love will lift us up and into the highest regions of our heart, we also fear the invariable "fall" when love departs and drops us back into a world left twice as dark for her withdrawal.

So keen to us are these recurring cycles of love won and lost, and their sense of loss so unwanted, that when love does come calling again our desire *to possess that which we love* has become all the greater. In some instances this longing can be overwhelming, and past painful experience prods us on to find some way to "own" this new love of ours. But, even if this feat were possible, we already have good reason to suspect that merely *possessing* what we love is impossibly incomplete. For what else have we been gradually learning through our relationships of the heart other than this one fact: *we are held ever apart from what we love by the very fact that we would clutch it to our breast.*

In our gradual discovery of what love would have us learn, we are gently directed to consider another kind of relationship with love; now we no longer yearn to be its possessor, *but rather to be possessed by it.* And so emerges, like a newborn infant within us, our first true notion of the idea of a Divine Love. Our earlier inclination to abandon ourselves to Love now becomes our need, for in the light of Love's revelations we can see, for the first time, how our own hungering identity — once viewed as being essential to our experience of love — is secretly Love's only impediment.

The often tragic stories woven around the classical and great historical Lovers of all ages attest to this essential stage of self-discovery, and anyone who has known such a consuming relationship knows something of the paradoxical relationship that Divine Love requires of her lovers. She requires that

we must lose ourselves within the secret wellspring of her supernal Love if we hope to find the true source of our own heart.
And so, gradually, in overlapping but well-defined stages, *Love
prepares the heart it wants, and the heart it takes is taught
Love.* The apprenticeship begins.

Love's teaching tames the wild heart; not leashing it, but
releasing it; not restricting it, but refining it to receive the freedom of fulfillment; a new kind of Freedom this heart is created
to bear and contain in its agreement to be conquered.

The heart without the mastery of Love is unbridled. Dry
and empty, coarse and crazy with thirst it runs. It hurts without knowing why, driven to consume without caring whatever
it may in the hope of a momentary respite from its own relentless stirring.

The heart subdued by Love surrenders itself and becomes
storehouse, pump-house, and storage line. It stands between
perfect fullness and complete emptiness, filling and being filled
by what has made it. Such hearts touch and are touched by the
unimaginable miracle of Love. Hearts such as these have no
need for hope of tomorrow because each has become the willing subject *and* domain of Forever.

This book is about that Timeless Journey the heart takes
when it is time for it to find the Heart that beats the drum in

us. Its words are the imperfect musings of an imperfect man moved along by his imperfect longing for Perfect Love. It is dedicated to those whose longing to know Love outweighs their wish to doubt its Timeless Life. They are the Heart's apprentices.

It is written for those who long to enter into the Light of this life more than they want to stand outside of it basking in the shadows of themselves. They are the heralds of the Light.

This book is sent out to find the poor who have awakened to find their heart is missing and who must now search it out even unto the endless Depths of themselves. They are the few whom Love has chosen.

If you are one of these few, then this book is written just for you.

~ GUY FINLEY

"Love is the magic that transforms all things into power and beauty. It brings plenty out of poverty, power out of weakness, loveliness out of deformity, sweetness out of bitterness, light out of darkness, and produces all blissful conditions out of its substantial but indefinable essence."

~ HENRY JAMES

I Don't Remember
Giving You My Heart

STEAL FROM ME MY WALLET, or even my name for what it is worth, and there's a better than even chance, if done smartly, I won't notice the theft until later. But doesn't it make sense that there would be *some* distinguishing feature of that instant when — from my very being — you took my heart?

After all, wouldn't a theft of this magnitude leave a telling mark of some kind? How could such a moment take place and the victim never know the crime against him — or in this instance, *within* him? The point is . . . I don't remember giving you my heart. Yet, this much is clear: it is in your possession.

Believe me, finding yourself with only an ache in the space where your heart used to beat is a very confusing condition, so much so that the search for it is the only constant I know. Compounding my uncertainty is that now I'm no longer sure just what to look for first: Is it my heart . . . or is it you I must find in order to be whole again? Is it the center of myself I search for . . . or do I seek instead the one who has left it so empty?

And where is the line between these two pursuits, *if* there's one to be found at all? Of late, it seems the answer to this mystery is even stranger than how I found myself in this condition to begin with.

For it occurs to me — as impossible as it has to be — that maybe, just maybe, *you are my heart* . . . and that maybe, just maybe, you always have been only I just didn't know any better.

Is it possible that one could be born with only a place for a heart? An empty space that can do nothing but wait to be filled with that which has always belonged to you? All these questions and — at least at this point — the only thing I do know for sure is . . .

I don't remember giving you my heart.

What Love Demands

I WAS THINKING THIS AFTER-
noon about the man who introduced you to me. What would I
say to him now, if we could meet?

Did he have any idea what he was doing?

Had he given any thought to what was going to happen to
me? How the rest of my life, every facet of it, would be shaped
by that moment our paths then crossed? Did he understand I
would lose everything I treasure because the only constant
value left for me to live for is to find you again?

As I look back now — in all fairness — I think he did know
. . . only I thought that *I* knew better.

For instance, I remember him telling me at the time that if I had any love other than a love for you that you would never truly be mine. Only what did I know — or care — back then? Nothing was any more real to me than what I wanted — and have you I would when and where it pleased me. How was I to know?

And it isn't that I'm trying to blame my trusted friend for my having lost my heart to you. That would be like finding fault with someone for offering you his finest wine — a rare vintage that, for its many subtle qualities, suddenly made all other wines known to you seem lifeless and without bouquet. All else aside, who can be blamed for what amounts to a change in my taste?

But this line between my heart's insatiable thirst and its sweet fulfillment in you is gradually becoming lost to me. I don't seem to know any more where one begins and the other ends — or if there ever was any real difference between the two? And maybe herein lies the answer to my original question concerning my old friend and whether he knew what he was doing on that fateful Day.

It occurs to me now, given my own predicament, that *he was already your consort*: as much a slave then to wanting to share his love for you — with me — as I now find myself enslaved to write these letters to you about my heart in your keeping. Each of us doing what we must within what your love demands; both fulfilling ourselves through fulfilling the hidden design of your unconquerable love.

The Perfect Fuel

T<small>HE WORD</small> <small>UNQUENCHABLE</small> has hidden meaning. Within it is secreted a whole and invisible text — one known, I suspect, only to those who have known a love such as yours. And now I have come to know its telling secret: For each day now I tell myself this search for you must cease, and even as my mind mutters these usual refrains, are my eyes straining for a glimpse of you!

What a strange madness this is! The thought of you consumes me at a depth I'm unable to influence.

I long to be like the log in my fireplace which burns so

bright but that, at last having spent itself in flames, is allowed to rest, transformed into that which can not be made to burn again. *What peace that must be.* And how I long for it.

But I find myself living in a flame that finds no such respite. Even when burning cold, *this* love can not be made to go out. No, it burns itself down to some determined end — where surely nothing is left save a buried spark — and then it flames all over again.

It's a terrifying thought that this kind of emptiness is such a perfect fuel; one that — even as it consumes itself — creates itself all over again.

Surely only you can quell this fire which burns on nothing, but that takes my all.

The Fire you seek

Burns within you.

The Light you long for

Longs there too.

To know yourself

And your heart's desire,

Embrace the Flame:

Let Fire be fire.

Half a Heart

W<small>HAT COULD BE WORSE THAN</small> to have only half of a Love-poet's heart?

Better to have none at all, I'm sure!

With half a heart, you know just enough to know that you're missing the other half; but the half that's missing is the one that finishes the rhyme and that transforms the awkward couplet into a perfected couple.

In half of a Love-poet's heart there's just enough passion to want to die for the Beloved, but not quite enough of it to finish the dance.

Half way in and half way out . . . neither fish nor foul . . .

the half-hearted Love-poet has but one wing. And though drawn to the water's edge cannot enter because he doesn't know how to fathom such depths.

Now do you see why I need you so? I'm flopping and flapping around out here, simple prey to hunters with no heart . . . and unable to find the rest of my own.

The Visit

I HEARD FROM YOU TODAY.

What's most strange is how sure I was this day would be different from all the others. Just imagine: waiting and wondering; loving you — resenting you — off and on, repeatedly, until the heart just wears itself out — until it wants to feel nothing at all.

So I guess the reason I'm surprised is because nothing in me feels like I thought it would. Nothing. Yet everything seems strangely in place. Maybe *quietly* in place is a better way to state my state . . . And I believe it is *this* quietness that's so strange.

After all, up until this morning, when I saw you, it felt as though I had been waiting for you forever. So wouldn't you think that at the moment of our reunion I'd hear some kind of marching band beating its way through my heart, or at least one victory speech? But no, there's nothing; well, not quite just nothing. It's a *deep* nothing. A very *rich* nothing having no comparison. Sort of everything and nothing all at once.

We will have to see how I feel in the days to come. After all, you couldn't stay.

At least that's what I told myself as you slipped away. But the truth is I feel fine, for the moment anyway. There is still something of you here with me as if you are not gone — even though you have.

Oh Quiet Light

This grateful heart

Sees you stealing into its room.

Unannounced, but welcome you are

To take whatever you might.

Your gentle stealth

Is no surprise,

And you enter upon your will;

So softly you remove the dark,

Replacing it with your Self.

Some Things Change,
Some Won't

Everything has its own
time. Everything, that is, except for learning that one all-im-
portant lesson that *everything in life has its own time!* If anything should be clear to me by now, this ought to be; but it's
just *not*.

The echo of my empty heart speaks louder than the rea-
soning of my mind; telling me that I'm not *really* alone — that
my forsaken feelings are only echoes themselves of footsteps
now past, and that I need only get back into step with the
changes of life. Such thoughts even make sense, after all . . .

For all living things *there is* a season for coming and going; moments of fulfillment followed by emptiness; a procession of starts and stops, of life and death.

Wouldn't you think that beings like ourselves — born from, and into, a world where ceaseless seasons are the only constant — that by now we would have made our peace with this parade that is our life?

Then why can't I accept that you've gone away?

Just Like That

SOMETIMES I JUST SIT AND LIS-
ten to the wind, watching its invisible fingers play with things
left there for its merriment. But I think that what most draws
me into its dance is that wind doesn't really start anywhere, or
end up in any one place. All of a sudden it is just here, there,
and everywhere; more in some places, less in others; moving
marooned things caught in its wake, while showing no signs
of the places it will lead them to and leave there.

Looking out of my window and watching freshly fallen
leaves dance out of sight into the approaching darkness, I imagine that a tree — having no idea what a wind is — must feel

about its visitations as do I your invisible comings and goings. The parallel feels too real: Suddenly something unknown comes along and gently stirs its branches with a touch so deft it leaves no trace of ever having been there.

And yet, barely scant moments later, this same gentle breeze can give way to a gale so unyielding that its unbridled force threatens to topple the tree.

And then, just like that . . . it disappears again with only the tremors in the tree as evidence that anything visited its limbs.

The only thing good about the stillness that remains is that it sets the stage for the next visit.

Your whole nature

Is here!

Not here!

Sometimes more of one

Than the other.

You come to me,

Then run

From me!

Keeping your secrets

From your lover.

Remembering to Never Forget

IF ONLY I COULD NEVER FOR-
get that I am without you — never find in your absence a moment of sweet respite — then I would never again be betrayed
by any of life's joys that life so callously left at my door. In the
light of this, my deliberate act of remembering never to forget,
each of life's deceptions would be seen as such, making it impossible not to recognize these merry moments for what they
are in reality: hopelessly incomplete . . . as are all moments
without you.

Do you think my interior posture too extreme? A closer
examination reveals its hidden and delicate balance.

How many times must I suddenly remember, *again*, that we are apart? More to the point, how often do I have to find myself embroiled in this ache of emptiness *before* I recall that I've *never* stopped *feeling* this way?

Perhaps it would be better for me if I never again felt any happiness, for what good is any brief ray of light if all it brings is a postponement of that inevitable darkness that persists in your absence? No, there is no pleasure in forgetting my heart's pain. For whatever joy may come, it is fleeting — like a sunny scene painted upon the rear curtain of a stage, little more than a backdrop that dresses a stark and otherwise empty space.

This afternoon I spent time listening to a stirring soundtrack from a past popular motion picture. Its music underscores the destiny of two lovers fighting to find one another in a world whose events have not only torn them apart, but that seems determined to keep them out of each others arms. I believe in such love stories great truths are revealed.

Throughout your continued absence I see that I have been looking for ways to live without you. I was wrong. This is the coward's path. I must learn to live while knowing that I am not fully alive — for without you there is no real life. Without the space molded in its center a cup can never hold what it is made for.

The Stubborn Hearted

I CAN NOT TELL YOU THE NUM-
ber of times — in the interest of peace of mind — that I have
decided to just be done with you and give up this search once
and for all!

But, as you've no doubt already noticed, this is an imperfect world at best. And as far as I can make out, it must have
had its unfortunate beginning in me. Take my heart for instance; it just doesn't get the message from my head.

Believe me, being stubborn hearted is much worse than being hard headed! With a hard head at least you can *eventually* learn. But with a stubborn heart you have to live with *its* refusal to stop looking for love — *your* love, to be specific.

Nevertheless, every day this heart of mine, despite my mind's protestations, beats afresh with the feeling like "today's the day!" As though *this* day will be different somehow from all the other empty days preceding it without you. And my heart isn't alone in this confusing internal conspiracy!

Even my eyes refuse to see it the way the rest of me would have this resolved. They too look for you every day, in every way, around every corner, as though they don't know their glance has yet to be returned in these many long years. But that's not the worst of it. My mind mocks my heart and its eyes.

"You have got to be kidding me," taunt my own thoughts. "What *are* you looking for?"

And, as always, too filled with high expectations to notice how it is being disparaged, too conscientious to turn around to see who is asking, my heart kindly answers: "I am looking for my Love!"

The Herald of Hope Unseen

I TRY CONVINCING MYSELF
that there's no point in continuing to think about you, but right
in the act I can see that trying *not* to remember you is just another way in which my mind dances in the dark around the
only light it sees there. Of course this faint and fading image of
you isn't really you, but such thoughts — and the hope they
hold out — may somehow herald your return. Perhaps this
kind of remembrance serves only sentiment, but there is evidence it does more than this.

I remember once, as a very small boy, a visit to a large de-
partment store where — to my childish horror — I found my-

self accidentally separated from my mother. At first, I didn't even notice that she and I had somehow wandered apart; but when I looked up at the adult face standing next to me — naturally searching for some consolation in my strange circumstances — hers was the wrong face! Definitely not my mother's! Then I turned to the next face, and the next in the crowd, and still no comforting smile fell upon me.

This terrible panic rose up in my chest. I recall feeling almost dizzy, heated, and disoriented. Seconds later, as if with a mind of its own, my small body began moving forward, pushed along by my own instinctual wish to find that one person with whom I knew I was safe.

But I was lost and being carried along in a current of my own urge — drifting through a sea of adult faces, none of which were right, and all of which, as they intruded into my upward straining line of sight, served only to make me feel more alone. I wanted only one thing: The face of my mother and the feel of my hand secure in hers.

Of course, looking back there was no way I could have known she was looking for me too. Such reassuring thoughts just don't occur to us in these tender years. Could I have only understood that she felt, as did I, there's no doubt I would not have felt so terribly afraid and vulnerable.

And now, recollecting this past event as my current condition directs me to, I only wish I could remember this one thing. Did we find each other that afternoon, or was it she alone who found me? Was I eventually cornered by some perfume lady or tie salesman and confined to wait in some "lost and found" section of the store? Or did I somehow, miraculously meet you "half-way"?

I think if I could remember I'd know what to do now.

Unexpected Rain

SOME MORNINGS, SUCH AS this one, I find myself filled with such a gentle love for you that I can't explain it to myself. Nor am I able to fathom how such a soft rain in my heart can wash away the weeks and months of hardness that gathers in me during your long absence. And yet, I am renewed.

What a mystery! For nothing has changed that I can see. I still don't know where you are, and you certainly haven't come to me.

Yet, please don't mistake my meaning. While this sweet-ness that overtakes me is beyond my comprehension, it *is not* beyond my deep appreciation. For each time you come to me in this unexpected fashion, I know that my day will go light, and that I'll think of you more often in the hours that follow.

And this remembrance, while it lingers, is alive. And so it makes me.

To Open the Eyes That See

Clearly THERE IS NO PEACE IN trying to forget you, so perhaps the answer to this affliction lies in refusing to accept a breath that doesn't take your name into my heart. Although I admit there is still some confusion as to the exact gain in this prescription, nevertheless there is some evidence of wisdom in it, and in that there is hope.

For instance, of late I've learned that my mind and my heart see things with different sets of eyes. And often, that how I am feeling in any given moment depends not so much on *what* it may be before my eyes, but rather upon which *part of me* is

active in this moment and doing this "seeing." This idea of
"what sees how" can be explained by the use of a simple example.

My mind, specifically my thoughts concerning you, looks
for you as a bee does a flower and with many of the same
hopes. Both search incessantly for somewhere to land, and
then to "know" this place by its supporting and nourishing
touch. Owing to these parameters — each time my thoughts
turn to find you, and discover you nowhere to be found — it
seems that I am able to touch nothing and that nothing touches
me.

On the other hand, my heart looks for you with eyes that
are able, at times, to behold you even though you are nowhere
to be seen. How this faculty works its miracle I can only yet
approximate, but I believe this to be near the truth of it:

There is something in the vision of the heart that loves that
allows her to see through the substances that separate her from
her longing, so that the barriers of space and time cease to ex-
ist in the distance between this beholder and its beholden.

The power within *this* order of perception is that unlike
my thoughts — which must first touch in order to know — the
heart comes to know its love through the very love with which
it would touch its lover. In other words, it seems that when-

ever I remember to give you my love, I receive your loving touch.

The love I have for you

Is what you've given me.

The hope I place in you

Is what you'd have me be.

The joy I find with you

Is what makes you happy.

The peace in knowing you

Is in you knowing me.

The Flicker That Would Be a Flame

THIS EVENING, WHILE READING another's account of his longing for his one, true Love, I couldn't help but be struck that my love for you paled in comparison . . . and here was the shock:

The impassioned heart, mine in this instance, believes itself to be incapable of any greater longing than itself can bear. But plainly there are greater hearts; heart's whose nature can not only endure greater depths of dark aloneness, but hearts which — in their deep forbearance — also realize those heights of love yet undreamed of by more timid souls such as my own.

Could it be that love comes only to those who love so greatly that they neither know, nor care, of their own consumption by its flame? And, if so, what of those of us in this world who have thought their flickering candle a great torch?

Still, I'm tempted to hope. There is an unspoken kindness in these findings — *if* we know where to look. For where there is only a little light there may yet be that flame into which love can come into its own fullness. And when it does, I know you'll be there.

Supernatural Ember

How many times have I de-cided to stop wondering about you and when you might re-turn, and felt there — in these same brief moments — a certain relief for my newly emboldened resolve? But the problem is that even as my mind delights in its own delirium, and man-ages to distract itself from this dilemma of where it is you've gone, my heart is not amused.

Nothing seems to sway it from its appointed course of longing for you — a condition which, by now, has become a total mystery to me. After all, why keep up this search for you?

I think to myself how pointless it all is, but apparently these thoughts are equally pointless, *and* powerless, for they can neither stop this longing nor dislodge it from my heart.

Like some supernatural ember that can't be cooled, this sense of emptiness glows on — rekindled again and again as if brushed over by some unseen breeze moving through the center of me. What a strange affair this is! Though freely do I admit my love for this too temporary light — as it alone remains to remind me of my wish for you — yet with each brief bright flaring I am made all over again the greater aware of the darkness within which this heart must now search.

Into the Arms of the Other Side

IT NEVER CROSSED MY MIND that I wouldn't be able to find and keep you. Such a thought had always been out of the question . . . that is, until now.

After all, I have been so near, so close to finding you so many times, it's always been beyond certainty that any other outcome — save our complete accord — was just not possible. This inscrutable knowing that we would be inseparably re-united has been the secret atomic structure of my life, so much so that around its electric promise did everything else about my life revolve.

But now this life-long certainty is crumbling, and with it so go pieces of me — loosed and flying off — into some unknown space never before seen except in dark dreams better off forgotten. And compounding this sense of deconstruction — born of the fear of what may not be — looms what *is*: a slowly spreading deadening; a deeply disconcerting recognition that what I have always taken as being *so* — just *isn't* so at all; that everything I had based my reason for being upon may, in fact, have no reason for being whatsoever. Like discovering that up isn't up and has always been down. Where does one turn? To what? It's almost too much.

If there's a happy ending to this journey, it's not clear who will be left to write it. I can feel the warmth of what little hope is left in me fading, setting quickly like the late-afternoon sun rushing to the arms of the other side.

Unlike Any Other Love

THERE'S JUST SOMETHING ABOUT mornings in autumn. What a wonderful time of the year it is when yellowing leaves are never not tumbling down from the trees, and the many sweet, small birds have begun returning from parts farther North to take their fill at my feeders.

This morning I was reading the personal account of another person who had the good fortune of spending time with you. And while hearing of such reports tends to make me feel jealous, or sad — owing to the fact that someone is far more fortunate than I am — my response on this morning was something altogether different and new.

In reading his experience with you, my own desire to be with you became so amplified that it broke back upon me; and there came over me a wave of love not only encompassing you and me, but it gathered into its irresistible wash this other lover of yours as well. There was no contest. We were all carried away together, perfectly.

What does this mean? Is it possible that I am to find myself loving those who love you as well? Such a thought would have been unimaginable up until today. But your Love is not like any other love, is it?

Love for the Sake of Love

LATE LAST NIGHT AS I LAY
there, sleepless and trying to quiet my usual thoughts of you,
once more the thought crossed my mind how tired I was of this
longing for you. Now the usual course of events on these rest-
less evenings is well known. Either I decide I can bear this aching for one more day — supported by the soothing hope of
your return — or I conclude that since you want nothing to do
with me, then so I with you. We are done, you and I, and that's
that!

Keep in mind that neither of these rescuing thoughts has ever actually changed one thing for me — or about us. That is, until last night when, right in the midst of these two plans, came a third thought such as one that had never before visited me. Here's what it brought to me there in my darkened room.

Even as I lay there, torn again between trying to reach some conclusive action that would bring an acceptable end to my heart's struggle, a thought something like this occurred to me: "Even if I could put you out of my mind, how do I stop loving you?"

And then came to me this utterly *other* thought. And though I have no certainty to such a claim, no way to prove it as being so, I think it sent by you. It said to my unspoken question of "how do I stop loving you" that I should not stop *loving* you but rather that I *should* stop.

I wasn't at all sure of what I was hearing, so I listened even more intently. Again I heard from there within me: "You don't stop loving *me*, but *you* must stop."

There was something to this strange idea. I could sense it. But what? So I waited, softly straining to see what shape was taking form in my mind. But it wasn't a shape forming there at all. In this message shined a Light and it reached into my darkened heart.

It wasn't as though a skyrocket burst upon a night sky or anything like that. But a quiet corner of my mind could now see beyond itself. Its vision was clear. And with the aid of these new eyes I saw that *no* ache for love is for *the sake* of love. Aches such as these are there only to confirm to the one who aches that *his* love is real.

It seems strange now to have been so convinced by my own seeming sincerity, but heartache is only secret self-love. In its endless longing this emptiness says it seeks an end to itself, and that it will succeed when it can, at last, empty itself into that missing heart of its affection. But this kind of emptiness doesn't seek anything except to spend another day with itself, for *this* is its *first* love.

And so I know now, in the light of this new understanding, that I can not have two loves. This is the secret meaning inside of last night's message: I'll only find you when I lose me. You will come when I go. I don't need to stop loving you to bring my heart its longed-for rest. I just need, somehow, to *stop being me* while loving you. It must be love, alone; otherwise it's not love.

One went to the door of the Beloved and knocked.

A voice asked, "Who is there?"

He answered, "It is I."

The voice said, "There is no room for Me and Thee."

The door was shut.

After a year of solitude and deprivation he returned and knocked.

A voice from within asked, "Who is there?"

The man said, "It is Thee."

The door was opened for him.

— Rumi

What Must Be Done

W HAT ARE YOU TRYING TO TEACH ME?

I feel like a child held captive in a college — attending lessons that are not only beyond his comprehension, but as though these instructions themselves pertain to life on some other world . . . where nothing I learn of it has any application to this one in which I dwell.

Must I be taught so? Must I understand these Laws of Love before I can enter their realm? Is it that no one walks through the world of Love without first being cleansed of his former world by the active principles of the New One? Could this dilemma of the heart — its unwanted education — be the mysterious enactment of that death said to precede Love's Real Life?

Yet for one who was once as dead, cut off from Life and blinded by self-love — whose eyes have been opened only to find themselves unable to see their unknown Redeemer — what choice is there but to walk where one is being led?

And so I follow. My only hope is *your* Goodness . . . for I know now, clearly, if there's ever to be any hope of my love mattering to *you*, then I can no longer dream of attaching any value to it *myself*. And this, of *all* your unknown ways, is by far the most difficult lesson to bear:

I am required to see that *without your love* my life is, in its entirety, nothing — a fact that brings the original lesson home, completing the circle. After all, how can someone who *is* nothing place value upon anything he has? For surely this value must be as imaginary as the thing it values. And yet, if this understanding is the cost, if this humbling of the heart is what you ask before you enter it, then I will do what must be done to pay the Price.

Vacant Space

THERE ARE STRETCHES OF TIME, moments within me where — as nearly I can tell — it seems I have no heart. No doubt this is a strange confession to make to you, my absent love, especially since you're not around to hear it! But then again, it's likely enough you already know of this strange condition.

Now I don't mean to say that I know myself as heartless — in the sense of being cruel or insensitive. I pray not! Though how one with no heart could hope to be kind is a difficult question indeed. Nevertheless, the better-suited word for these times of heartlessness is simply lifeless.

Now if you've never known your own moments without a heart, this kind of lifelessness has to be the strangest of all possible experiences life can offer. When it occurs you don't even care that you don't have a heart with which to care about your own heartless condition! In moments such as these the way that you know you are still alive is because you can still feel life's basic effects. You breathe, you see, you taste, you hear, and you touch. And yet, *this* life . . . is lifeless.

One is sentient, even alert, but all quietly and so terribly void of reason for being at all. Neither is this state of oneself some kind of an emptiness that steals into the heart to rob it of the rhythm of life.

It's far more intangible than that — something akin to the feeling one gets when gazing upon that standing vacant space that's left behind when something cherished that was once there is no longer there.

At least an *empty* heart knows itself to be alive, even if it's only for its own aching. So I stand by my earlier claim: I have no heart. And while I don't remember giving it away (after all, who in his right mind would agree to that!) I am sure it is in your possession. What's left of me is this knowledge that I am the possessed.

The Price One Must Pay

SOMEHOW, AND EVERY DAY BE-
coming more apparent than is to my liking, I know that your
absence from my life is less a question of your love for me than
it is of mine for you. And this intuition tears at me because
though I think to myself that I want to do so . . . how can I
possibly ever love you as perfectly as you would have me do?
Experience tells that either my purse-like heart is too small, or
the price of perfect love must be more than I know how to pay.

And yet! How can this be? After all, not having the price
to pay is one thing. Not being *willing* to pay another.

Can it be I've lied to myself all these years? That it's not *you* withdrawn from me, but *me* withdrawn from you — having wandered away and become lost in some unseen sentiment whose once sweet content now leaves me so strangely discontent?

It seems implausible and yet, in spite of the pain of what has been this perennial longing, the evidence speaks well. And though difficult to endure, still I must listen to what your prolonged absence tells.

What's this I hear?

. . . That what has been at the center of my own heart all this time has been *me?* It's really too much to imagine! But with what I know to be true of your Love, there can be no other explanation for my emptiness.

At least now I know where not to look anymore.

Before I dream may I hope for you.

Before I long may I reach for you.

Before I judge may I listen to you.

Before I rush may I rest with you.

Before I shout may I call on you.

Before I doubt may I hear from you.

Before I brag may I point to you.

Before I fear may I trust in you.

Before I act may I remember you . . .

So that in these things, in all I do,

It is not me that is first, but always you.

The Edge of Love

To the casual glance the idea of love and "madness" would seem two totally different creatures: the case for love being where one longs to possess the object of his heart; the latter case being where one's mind is possessed or occupied by a presence whose will imposes itself upon his own, subjecting this person to *its* longings.

But what happens when Love brings a person to an impossible edge between these two worlds and leaves him there to let some unearthly gravity decide his fate? And more tellingly, what is the difference between these two worlds if one is secretly the cause of the other, as I now suspect it to be? Small wonder then as these lines blur that he can no longer discern which is which: Is he losing his mind or fulfilling the dictates of his heart?

For instance, all day today — regardless of who I was with — all I could feel was this overwhelming wish that instead of it being *me* who was looking out from behind my eyes — that *somehow* — it could be *you* doing the seeing.

I could not stop wanting it to be you who was listening through my ears to all those people who — even as they spoke — never knew I wasn't listening to them but for the sound of your voice in their own. And so wherever I went there was this overwhelming feeling that would neither go away nor be fulfilled . . . where my one desire was that instead of me living out my life, it would be your life living in me. If this is madness, it's your doing.

Strange Days

THESE LAST SEVERAL DAYS HAVE been harder than usual. There's a strange emptiness to their passing and this sensation runs through me as well. We both seem void of purpose, without will to proceed. And I can't blame this sacked state of myself upon its most familiar friend: you. The truth is that in these same days I have felt strangely empty of wanting to think about you at all. But what I find the strangest of all — even as I remain here unmoved by any longing for you — is that I am sure the reason nothing moves in me *is because of you.*

How it is possible for something *to be* and *to not be* at the same time? It's not, but here are the facts: Of late I haven't had the heart to think about you at all, to hope for you in any way. And yet . . . my heart's own absence is an emptiness that speaks *only of you.* In effect, I am made to hear the voice of . . . nothing.

I'm not sure what death is to be like, but if it commences with a call from lesser nothing to come into greater nothingness, I shouldn't fear too much. For on my appointed day I will know that threshold as having stood there before.

Before the waters come,

A well must hold its emptiness.

Before the mountains rise,

They wait in silent lowliness.

Before a sound is played,

The reed wraps round its hollowness.

Before a soul knows Life,

It must embrace these passing deaths.

The Love of Winter

IT ALWAYS AMAZES ME ON SUN-bright mornings such as this one how I could have ever forgotten just how much beauty hides in a winter day. The ground is covered in rich brown tones borrowed from curling leaves. Here and there pop up patches of fall-parched grasses just greening, reborn from early rains. And, more than anything else, the stark trees of winter stand like nature's exclamation points.

How I love the trees of early winter, so sparsely dressed in their few remaining leaves, barely hanging on otherwise barren limbs. Their collective voice speaks in a brusque tongue of richer days gone by and of colder days to come.

But it's the unspoken story these bared trees tell that helps warm and strengthen me most. For when the trees are full, and green, theirs is a story *already* told.

Of course they can be put through an unknown dance by late summer winds, or catch the last moments of the setting sun and stand there, shimmering, in contrast to their own strange shadows. But even so, *all that they are is in sight*. And *this* is why I love trees in winter: With their last garments of green removed, I feel more intimate with them, as though neither of us can hide anything from one another.

And even though it may be a subtle one, I confess to feeling a certain hope in seeing this forgotten state of theirs. For if it's true that in this pure barrenness there dwells such honest beauty — and that this beauty has always been there — only hidden for the time — then perhaps your absence isn't what it appears to be but only serves to reveal another form of your love.

Does this last thought sound too much like barren hope struggling for a new spring? I know it is not!

If trees move through seasons — and their loveliness only

changes to reveal itself in new forms — then why not consider that Love has Her seasons too? And is any season more beautiful than another, or is it just that we tend to forget those very special elements each has to offer in its own time and on its terms?

Is spring greater than winter? Summer more important than fall? Don't they really need one another in order to be all that they are?

So, for today anyway, I find great beauty in your absence. For now the presence of your promise in me is felt more keenly than the residue of these last barren seasons. No, I don't see you; and it's quite clear that I don't know where you've gone. Still . . . and in spite of all this evidence . . . or perhaps for the very lack of it . . . I know that you are here.

You and Only You

ONE THING *IS* FOR SURE — AT least for today, anyway. I can not begin to explain why I feel *as good as I do*. It isn't right. I shouldn't! This state of myself makes no sense whatsoever. And before you judge me too harshly — for what seems an unpardonable unwillingness to accept this happiness — my reticence can be explained, even if never fully understood!

My last words last night, before a compassionate sleep came to carry me off, were a prayer that I might be allowed to die. Mine was as sincere as any sentient creature might be al-

lowed to make this wish. And even though I feel content today, almost happy, verging on being over-confident — the *fact*
remains the same: I don't want *this* life — or any other for that
matter — without *you*. But, like everything else in this strange
relationship of ours, what I want carries very little weight.

All day yesterday, through and up until last evening, all I
could find working in my heart was my deepest certainty yet
that I have nothing of you save lost hope. And although I did
happen to speak with someone about you in great length this
morning, there was no change from the night before: I did not
wake up with you; no message from you was waiting at my
door; nothing stirred anywhere. So what on earth is this vi-
brancy that I feel?

I know this makes little sense, if any at all, but I don't want
to be happy if this happiness isn't because of you.

I don't want to feel strong — or secure — if this strength
of character is built upon anything outside of you. I want none
of it because I know it's illusion; a coincidental alignment of
internal conditions and stars; a temporary sun-burst because
circumstances allow it, secretly confirming some deeply-
seeded unseen self interest of mine. But stars and circumstance
change. They dance to music that changes tempo and key
without notice.

Only you are eternal. Only your love lasts. This is why I don't want the day's happiness . . . because if you aren't behind it . . . it isn't really happiness at all.

Let not my sadness spoil this Sorrow,

Nor appetites displace this Hunger for you.

Let not my crying stain these Sweet Tears,

Nor staid oblations steal the Need to be True.

Let nothing remain but this Native Need,

So where ever I am or what I may do

I can not help but to remember

Life is given to me, but I am made for You

My Foolish Heart and I Agree

MY MIND IS CROWDED THIS gray morning with sluggish, unyielding thoughts. Relentless in character they seem less the usual avalanche and more glacier-like; pushing and shoving chunks of confusion and me in their heaving midst with no place to hide that isn't part of their movement; carried along in their flow to who knows where, let alone why. Such is the terrain of myself without you in it. Which is why . . .

On mornings such as these I'm compelled to write about you. Perhaps hoping to find — in some previously unconsidered thought of you — a moment of high ground like a rock to stand on in the middle of a fierce river, or an island's sheltering harbor, tucked safely away from these maelstroms in myself.

Then again, and more likely, maybe these passages of the heart are written *to* you . . . conceived in the secret hope that somehow you'll receive their message and, hearing of my plight, cross that unknown distance between us to pull me out of myself.

Of course these invitations have yet to work, at least as hoped for in their moment of making! It would seem that considerations of the heart such as these are always the last to recognize their own fallibility. Perhaps it is just as well. My foolish heart and I agree: It is better to call out to you than to dwell in the bitterness of believing you out of reach.

Only Smoke and Water

M<small>Y</small> LONGING FOR YOU MUST be consuming itself for as far as I can tell there remains in me nothing left for it to burn. I feel no fire.

And yet, there is smoke and my eyes water.

I am at a loss. What kind of longing is this? It neither dreams nor seeks; it doesn't *do* anything except leave me numb to everything; that is to say everything *except* for this unwanted feeling of feeling unwanted.

It must be that buried somewhere in this ancient mud of myself something smolders. And even though none of its heat reaches the surface, everything there within me is under its effect. Nothing grows. Nothing lingers. No fragrance. Barely lit. Is the barrenness of this country *because* of you — or is it barren there, *here* in me, in readiness *for* you?

Please, won't you send some word? *If* there is no sweet difference between these two inner conditions, as profess the saints-of-Love, then I've missed it just as I am still missing you.

Dismantling Me

Each evening just before sleep comes to carry me away, and then again in the dawn of almost every morning, I ask for you to grant me my heart's desire: to end this emptiness that earmarks every page of my life.

For the record let it be said that you *do* come.

You *do* fill in these estranged places in me . . . but only to take them away, something akin to granting a person asylum on a ship that is sinking one piece at a time.

This morning you came and when you left you took away my longing for you. But not by its soothing, as you've often done for me in the past. No, this morning you stole it, outright. You told me that it's impossible for me to long for you as *you* are: that this ancient tugging in my heart *is not* about needing you for your sake, but for my own — for what I believe your love will do for *me*.

There was nothing I could say. Right is right.

Then you told me that *this* kind of love isn't yours, and can never be.

Again I was silenced. Nothing was everywhere. Then you were gone and — with you — went yet another part of me.

What kind of love is this? I simply can not have enough of you and it is dismantling me.

I want to pour myself into you,

No backwaters:

Straight, strong, deep, slow,

Indifferent where this flow

Takes me.

Let there be no record of this love,

Like waters erase themselves

In their own surge.

Speak to me. No intimations,

But in words direct.

Not reflection, not perception,

Shatter this dam.

Lovers Passing By

IT BEGAN IN EARNEST EARLY this morning; although looking back I can see this feeling actually started several weeks ago. By late afternoon I was barely able to contain myself. How I wanted to tell someone — anyone! — of my ecstatic heart; and yet who would understand? In truth, my condition is strange even to me given that I haven't seen you, or had word from you, in what seems the longest time.

Still, for weeks my heart has held you near, though not in ways easily described.

It's been a distant fashion — familiar, but removed — where you've been missed, but not really longed for. Sought after, but almost like looking for something sweet to round out a perfect meal.

That's why today is so extraordinary. For I can't say where you are, because by evidence you're nowhere around and yet, by heart, you must be present . . . so near that what you are touches me.

I've seen a few select movies where lovers pass one another by, neither glimpsing that the other is right there, yet each knowing that their love is close because their hearts can see what their eyes aren't able to. This is how I feel today, right now: as though you're standing just to the side of me — so near — but somehow outside my line of sight.

I wish others could learn how extraordinary your love really is. How it can just disappear, be seemingly lost for months, even years on end and then, from out of nowhere, return to fill this — its absent heart — with the unmistakable notion that it was never really gone and that all emptiness is . . . little more than an illusion of Love.

The Way It Is

I SAW YOU TODAY. WHAT amazes me most — within each of these too brief visits — is how being with you always shows me another of the mistaken ideas I have and hold — about *myself*.

For example, in times when neither you nor my heart are anywhere in sight, it feels to me as if I don't possess a thing. This sense of inner poverty can be so pervasive that I no longer care I'm *this* close to never caring about *anything* again — let alone despairing that both you and my heart are missing. My certainty is almost settled and then . . . you appear.

In what feels an infinite instant I am not just brought back from the brink of the abyss, but find myself dancing along its edge! Suddenly I am more than alive — in the throes of a quickening that *again* carries me beyond caring — only this time to the *other* side of the chasm. I ask myself . . .

How is it possible to be as helpless *within* your love . . . as I am *without* it? And I think I hear you say, "That's just the way it is."

Loving Is Being Loved

THERE IS SO MUCH THAT NEEDS to be done today, but I can't do anything other than sit here, wonder where it is you have gone with my heart, and long to be with you as in our yesterday.

It is an extraordinary thing — this engaging feeling that comes with simply remembering you — even though I have no idea where you are. How is it possible to feel such an abiding tenderness for what I am unable to see? Let alone touch or possess? And yet!

On mornings like today with such soft winter sunlight gliding through the bared branches and the air so cool and undisturbed, I'm moved to embrace the thought that it is enough just to feel the way I do.

Actually, it occurs to me on days such as these that it is in the loving that one finds love.

With all things I can serve Thee,

In all things I can find Thee,

Through all things I can know Thee,

For all things I can love Thee.

The Sand of Myself

THERE ARE TIMES WHEN BEING with you — like this — that I can't help but imagine how the desert must feel in a last minute late summer rain.

From above you fall in life-giving drops on to sands so dry they swell even with the promise of your approach.

And like the sand that must mourn the stuff of itself — that can do nothing but draw tenuous sips from rain waters before they slip away, I wish — as you pour yourself out to me — a small pool might form, a puddle to somehow capture and hold your life-renewing love.

Where do you go once beneath this sand of myself? How can mere sand ever know the secret of the Rain?

Maybe that's what love is all about.

The Message

Looking out my picture window on this white-gray January morning and watching the first snowflakes of the season drift down to slowly cover the ground, floating along with them is this one thought that sits almost suspended before my eyes.

I can tell this gentle vision wants me to look away from my thoughts *of* you so that it might show me something *about* you. Its silent reflections tell me I have been mistaken in my relationship *with* you . . . and that outside of this misunderstanding on my part there are no obstacles to our Love.

I get the message.

Think of it: The only basis by which we deem ourselves suited to stand in judgment of another's actions towards us is according to how well *we think we know* that person. Suddenly it all seems too clear. How else could we, *so* knowingly, determine the goodness, or lack of it, in any person's behavior towards us other than to pit it against some foregone conclusion of our own making?

This finding shows us that an unseen but definite relationship exists between *what we think we know* about someone and *the level of disappointment* we feel with regards to that same person. In other words, we can only feel as bad about how someone else treats us as we feel ourselves certain, or knowledgeable, about them.

When we ask — as forlorn-feeling lovers often do — "How could you leave me alone for so long?" . . . or, "Why didn't you send word of your whereabouts?" . . . or, "What makes you treat me this way?" . . . we ask because, in *our* heart, we believe we *know* the one we ask. Could it be that this sense of the familiar — this same knowledge we believe we possess of the other — is the culprit that creates our unrealistic expectations *and* their subsequent painful dashing? Without these unconscious demands, where is the sting of our disappointment?

Besides . . . Where did I ever get the idea I *know* you? If anything the facts are that *everything* you've ever done for me — or given to me — has taken me completely by surprise, only deepening my sense of wonder and uncertainty as to the nature of your character! So much so that the only true certainty I possess concerning your Love is how perfectly I continue to misjudge that Great Mystery which seems to be the center of your Soul.

So the truth is although I *do* love you with all of my heart, I *do not* know you. Not really.

What I do know now is that your Love has no substitute. It does not have an address. Your Love can't be a place that *I* can go to and visit — otherwise such knowledge turns into familiarity followed by forgetfulness, and finally, unfaithfulness.

Looking back for a moment, as such illuminations make possible, now I can see that *I only* thought *I had to know you* . . . as though something in this "knowing" of you would somehow make you more mine. But now I see that it's been this very demand *of mine* that alone is responsible for darkening and delaying our love. In the clarity of this discovery, it seems silly to have ever thought otherwise.

After all, I love the silence in a deep snowfall . . . and I don't *know* snow! And how I love the spring antics of the birds on the leaf-strewn forest floor . . . and I don't *know* the first thing about foraging for nesting materials or seed!

I only thought I knew you, and you've been trying all along to show me that I don't . . . and need not. After all, your Love is a *Visitor.* She must be received unannounced and in unknowing. Such a relationship is not a question of agreement but of surrender. Which I do.

To Find You

CERTAINLY NOT EVERY MORN-
ing, but in more of them than I care to explain to myself, I try
to find some way to empty myself of this constant emptiness
that my life is like without you. But it's beginning to dawn upon
me that for all of the ways I have found to pour out my heart,
this does little to fill its need and, apparently enough, nothing
noticeable to entice you closer to me. All of which begs the
question: What good is this continual emptying out of my emptiness?

After all, only a fool struggles to delay the inevitable, like a man trying to sweep back the sea with a broom to keep it from washing over him. And speaking of going under comes to mind a question I've never considered before:

Would **complete** emptiness know itself as being *fully empty* . . . or as *completely full*? And perhaps even more important than this question — whose answer can only be found through experience — is there any **real** difference between the two? I fear I must find out before I am to find you.

A Friend in Need

ONE OF THE REASONS I FEEL so alone on days such as these is that when you're not with me there's just no one else to talk to about my love for you. Please don't think this unreasonable on my part. After all, who but you can understand what you have made of me?

Certainly *I* don't understand it: this obliterating obsession; these times when my every heartbeat feels as though the next one will be my last one unless you appear. And then . . . you don't, but *still* I survive.

But these are just weary words spoken into emptiness from hollowness. *This* is why I wish I had a Friend to talk to: someone who understands that there are some words hidden too deep in the heart that — if ever given wing — only turn graceful swans into ugly ducklings. Someone who — listening to me *not* speak still hears everything I've said . . . and then says so in that silence only Lovers can understand . . . as it is when you and I are together.

Love Finds Whom She Will

I REMEMBER READING ONCE, and being so struck by its substance, that when it comes to a Love such as ours, there is one inescapable rule: *There is nothing any lover can do of his own accord that will bring to him that Love for which he longs.* But once the sincere seeker understands this — his own impotence — he must (if he wishes to find his missing Heart) then forget that he knows this Truth! And it is in this forgetfulness, I fear, that I have succeeded too well!

Every day, without fail, I set out to find you and make you mine, oblivious to the unspoken Law governing Lovers until

— as most days rule — I find only myself. Then I shuffle off to try and find you again — not unlike some needful toddler who, missing his mother, goes to her bed after she has risen, hoping for a hint of what little warmth or scent of her remains in its coverings — searching for the one who loves him as no other.

Yet the allure in this, my daily quest for you, is greater than my power to resist; and this is in spite of the fact that, for the most part, all I find at its end is myself unfulfilled. And even though I know well this immutable Law that governs all seekers — that Love finds only whom She will . . . still, it seems to me that, somehow, we *do* meet in this way. That setting out to be with you — as I do every day — somehow sets the stage for being with you.

Besides, there is this fear that if I don't seek you out, my heart will be lost to you forever wherever it is that you have gone without me. And I don't want to die without my heart even though most of the time that's the way it already feels.

What More Can You Ask

I'M NOT SURE WHY IT WORKS
out this way, but some mornings are better than others. Maybe
it's because in mornings such as these everything just seems to
come together in the right proportions — at just the right moment — to remind me of you. Take this morning for instance.

Sitting before the fireplace to ward off the early chill of a
pre-spring dawn, I was holding my mug of hot coffee to my
chest. This is something I often do.

The mug's gentle heat not only comforts me through the
cloth of my robe, but it passes through my body and delivers

its warmth to my welcoming heart. This little ritual brings me comfort because, in its own gentle way, it helps me remember what you mean to me: Life.

Maybe this sounds silly? A grown man clutching a mug of coffee to his chest to warm his heart in the absence of the one he loves! Be that as it may, as I sat there relishing the warmth of mug, fire, and my hope in you, the sun broke out and sent its beams streaming through the thick, low-lying fog that is peculiar to this time of the year. What a light is that light which pierces the grayness!

It seems to me that somehow, whenever the sun finally breaks through a fog-choked morning or fully clouded afternoon sky, its light is that much brighter — as though the rays themselves were joyous for their victory over the gloom!

Whatever the case, that's how it was this morning: A celebration of sunlight poured into my house and filled it just as the warmth from my mug spread over and into my heart. And for a moment I had it all. It was as though you were right there with me.

What more can you ask of any morning?

Such Is Your Love

YOUR LOVE . . . IS SUCH, AND I have seen . . . that in a space of fifty minutes, while never having once left it, you can reinstate yourself in my heart fifty times.

In each of these tender renewals you make me feel as though never has there been such a perfect reunion as in that last one minute: where over and over again you and I are together for the first time . . . as though there has never been such a moment before. How this is possible I can't begin to guess. But . . . such is your Love.

And if I am the fool for this Love — or somehow I'm being fooled by what is my own love for yours — then let me go on being the greatest fool that ever lived. Only let me live in Love.

You are the uncharted melody,
The grace notes no one knows to the Song of Life
Until You suddenly sing some delicate new measure
through the Soul.

Then is born a music that makes every note thereafter
As if one never heard before.

Melody and counter melody in a balance so fine that each
becomes the other.
One variation upon another, weaving, inter-penetrating,
Until disappearing into themselves.

And with each brief, pristine passage
Is born a whole new Song:
Giving, in turn, birth anew
To the one who hears You sing.

Remembering

There are many days when even the simple act of holding the thought of you is beyond my power to do. And while there is little enough comfort in just being able to remember you . . . at least with the thought of you held fast in mind . . . my heart seems less disturbed by your absence.

But it should be said that this — my inability to hold on to your company inwardly — isn't for lack of desire on my part. I *do* want to be with you even if — in these lesser times — all I have of you to share is my own recollection. So my feeling of helplessness here, in being unable to remember you, is hard endured. When I don't have you, the me I have to be with . . . I don't want to be. Or, at least, that's what I always thought was the truth. However, more recently, I've been seeing a certain self-contradiction — a fact about myself that this same self is hard-pressed to explain away.

Whenever I can somehow remember that I've forgotten you — *the one I want to remember above all else* — instead of surrendering myself to the promise of being renewed by the returning thoughts of you — I become fascinated with the depths of my own shallowness. Rather than reaching out for *your* presence, I see myself secretly embracing *itself*; commiserating with itself about its inconstancy; weeping over what it calls its own darkness that must somehow be endured as the price to be paid for your love.

And though the answer has already told itself, I am made to ask the following question: Who is it that I *really* love? A question that, in itself, leads us on to an all-but-forgotten ancient Truth. It *is* true. We **cannot** love *two* things.

So, regardless of appearances . . . And oh! How cleverly they may be kept . . . there can be but one conclusion: Myself loves only myself. It cares only for that too familiar thrill of itself. **This** is *its* love. The evidence before me speaks louder than the doubts myself calls to its defense. And yet . . . in spite

of how dark seems this new discovery, there is in it a great Light
. . . one that holds, curiously enough, as much bright promise
as it also serves to confirm what is perhaps the oldest teaching
about the nature of True Love.

For despite all the doubt this newest darkness brings to
bear, there remains no doubt that still do I love you. Or — perhaps better said in the new light being brought to bear — that
you so love me that I'm aware of *your Love in me*. This fledgling Love I've taken as mine *really belongs to you* . . . Which,
of course, makes it all the more precious.

For clearer than ever before is that your Love is the only hope
I have of escaping the circle of my own, small self love . . . leading me to newly resolve that I will increasingly strive to remember two things: the *first* of which will be *you*.

The second thing I will remember . . . upon my being
able to remember you . . . is just how important it is to *forget
myself*.

Let Me Run With You

SOMETIMES WHEN YOU RUSH in, I feel as though I am standing upon the bank of a river rising up in me, and that you are its sudden waters coming over me.

Caught up as I am in these moments, all I want is to be carried away. I want to offer myself, toss myself into this upwelling; but I don't know where to find the edge of these waters in order to leap.

In these times I feel as the parched earth must know the summer squall — its too brief downpour racing over worn runways of thirst-stricken soils. *And I want to run with you.* Wherever it is you go, I want to run with you . . . for this mere swelling of my soul-substance is not enough!

If the waters of a summer's storm can carry in their course mountain rocks to the great lake below, then surely there must be a way for me to run with you.

There is a storehouse of Sanity,
A vault of Love,
A treasure of Kindness,
All bursting at their seams.

Can't you feel the pressure
To just be Light?

Don't the walls of your heart
Ache to break loose and open
The floodgates of Freedom?

You have riches untold,
But have lost the map to the upper regions of yourself
Where you are always overflowing.

So, forget this world with its intermittent streams
Whose waters begin and end.
Search out the Ocean, and stand in Her surge
Until the waves wash away the shores of your soul.

The Wind and Mountain Lake

WHAT ELSE CAN I DO? I KNOW that my behavior *without you* speaks far louder than do my words when you are *around me*, but it *is* true nevertheless: In my heart I don't want to make the smallest demand upon you. After all, what say do I have over the smallest aspect of your Life!

Still, asking for you, wanting you always near, just seems to come naturally; because when at last you've come to me, when I am with you, *every* little thing is with me.

Whatever I behold feels quietly held . . . as a high mountain lake holds its mountain's image without shudder or heave. With you . . . I want for nothing more. The picture is complete . . . so much so . . . that in these Timeless times nothing occurs to me to be done, and its perfect reflection is that nothing in me moves to do anything. And should more of this nothingness rush in — as it will sometimes want to do — even *this* most feared and formidable foe falls on its knees before *you*, content to be what it is. Which only makes perfect sense when you are here.

After all . . . what is the power of any wind compared to the permanence of mountain and lake?

Now I know we are one come together . . .
Like the seasonal branch
from its perennial vine do I rise

Just as Ever are You, so in passing am I . . .
Yet no sorrow mars this spring nor stays its indelible mark

And when this brief season closes
and makes each branch to fall . . .
Still I will find no fear within you
for what is a branch . . . But the Vine after all

To Gather and Scatter

I AM ALWAYS SURPRISED BY YOUR strength — by how happy I am to be too weak to do anything except completely accept you. What is this power of yours? How shall I understand it?

Are you a Gathering Force?

When you come, do you collect all the parts of me that have wandered off high and low looking for you . . . somehow drawing them all into one place wherein their deep peace is that they once again know that they need never look for anything beyond being drawn into your gentle holding?

Or is your strength a secret Scattering Force?

Have you the power to dissolve everything? To unglue the stuff of even my most tenacious thoughts and send them back into their native nothingness . . . so that I too disappear . . . except for where your will acts as a New Nucleus softly holding an unknown me in the Heart of an unknown Core. In this pure and unknowable Place I both am — and am not; and the strength therein is that I could not care less which case is true!

This is *your* strength: It absorbs, without concentrating. It looses, without losing. So . . . it *is* true: Only Love makes everything, nothing . . . and makes nothing, everything. Only Love. Only You.

Only a Pauper's Love

IT IS FAIRLY CLEAR TO ME *NOW*:
There are rules surrounding this kind of Love that do, indeed, determine its fruition or failure — but *these* rules are set by the one sought after, never by the seeker.

Most of my considerations amount to little more than the continuing unconscious constructions of an unrequited lover: Someone who thinks his foremost wish is to please his Beloved, but whose daily acts of contrition are both fueled by, and conceal, one surging self-centered emotion after another . . . acts of longing designed not so much to please his Beloved, as they are to fill himself.

In other words, he struggles not to keep alive the Love he claims to live for, but rather *his* love of longing.

In this person there is no act of self-abandonment for the sake of his beloved that isn't a simultaneous secret act of self-adornment. Small wonder then that all along you have been trying to tell me — asking me, really — to understand one thing: Before I can hope to know your Love, fully, my own love must first become as worthless to me.

Otherwise this same love ferments the self, pumps it up and intoxicates it with secretly self-injected measurements of what it holds so dear about itself — a daily source of an undetected self-adulation that (by its very nature) prohibits me from giving my heart away with complete abandonment. And you ask for nothing less.

The Way to your Heart is very clear. It's only when this love of mine is fully impoverished that it becomes priceless; for it is this poor love, this pauper's love, that alone pleases you.

Slowly I Turn

WHENEVER YOU COME TO ME I have no questions for you, only openness. Nothing needs be spoken. Everything is in its place; all is accounted for.

But when you leave . . . I am like a harbor without a boat; a nest without a bird; a cup that somehow knows what it means to have capacity, yet that sits without any means to fill itself except for this flood of questions rushing to pour themselves into where you once were.

What is it about you? How is it that your footsteps through my heart — even on their way out — leave only imprints of a new promise?

What is in your hand that can touch my soul almost imperceptibly, yet move it so much?

How do you speak to me of all that matters without ever saying a word? Coming out of the darkness, going into it, and then back out again almost unannounced, save the sudden sense of awakening light left there in your place? What is it about you?

It would not be too hard to imagine how, long, long ago before men and women had learned that the earth revolved, turning herself around the sun, that with the close of each day they would huddle together, trembling, asking amongst themselves, "Where has the great light gone to? What did we do to cause the warmth to depart? Will it return?"

One can almost guess how these early nights of our distant ancestors would be filled with a certain apprehension — for what if the light of their lives chose never to return again!

Of course such questions seem silly now . . . after all, the sun never quits the sky but only waits for the earth to turn and face the light.

I am in love
With what has begun,
I am in love
With what Love has done.

I am in love
With the Living Sun,
In whose Perfect Light
Perfect Love is won.

The Wish to Be Known by You

LET ME DWELL WITH YOU BUT for this moment . . . and have you as you give yourself, not as I would try and take you.

Here, now with you, it is clear your love is endless, and that I deny myself your ecstasy by looking for crude possession — trying to hold fast to the blunt end of my comprehension of you, when I have seen that even to call out your name sends you away. Your love is beyond knowing, even though its instructions are chiseled in my heart.

This incessant seeking to understand you has not been to love you the more, as I have given myself to believe, but more to gain and hold some imagined upper hand: to possess you even as a man would capture and tame some wild creature through feigned kindness with the end in mind of using its strengths to ease his burdens.

In this I have been wrong — not to you, but to myself. If one thing has become clear it is that there can be no understanding your supernal Love — much as I admit this fact troubles my natural mind. Yet, seen aright, even this disturbance brings me nearer to this Peaceable Presence of you. After all, one of the reasons any such mind seeks *to know* the object it holds is because whatever is known to it in *this* way it comes to take as being its own; and *you* are possessed by nothing save your own unknowable nature.

There can be no mistake, even though I continue to make them: The one great lesson is that there can be no knowing your love, only the moment to moment surrendering of myself should I wish to be known by you.

That soul by love unleashed wills to descend,

To pierce in gentleness through every fabric and veil

Until it reaches its own unraveling.

And there . . . undone, to linger unknowing,

Being carried along in timeless tides

Where its longing to be intimate with the Infinite

Is quieted at last.

With Every Beat

IT SEEMS TO ME ON THIS LATE spring afternoon, sitting here watching the sun quietly retrace its steps over greening fields — that I love you as much for what I've been given to know of you — as for what I know in my heart I have yet to be told. Yes, I'm sure of it: The only thing greater than this fledgling love are the secrets it has yet to reveal.

Even unrequited (as it so often turns to be) such love is glorious. It fills the heart as air refreshes the lung. Only in this love

of ours — in its moment — there is no out-breath, no need for
release to refresh itself. Sweeter still the longer it remains, this
love is like drawing in a deep breath of blossom-enriched air,
and then being able to linger with that soft scent, undiminished
for its partaking. This is your love. And I thank you with every
beat of my stolen heart when, as now, it is so swollen with the
scent of you.

How I've longed for the scent of You,

So I dare not disturb this air

For softly now it comes over me,

Your sweet silence everywhere.

As You Please

THIS LATE SUMMER MORNING, while I was out walking and thinking about you — as I am often so inclined to do — it occurred to me that whenever you do appear to me, I never pause to consider *where* have you just come from? Nor does it occur to me to ask you *why* is it that you have come to me in the moment that you have chosen?

And yet . . . each time you depart . . . all I do is question why you had to go away, and then torment myself over where it is that you've gone!

Why should your dreaded disappearance be a greater mystery to me than your sudden and longed-for arrival?

Why should the departure of anything in life be of greater consequence than its coming, especially when you know nothing of its origin or destination?

Doesn't the wind come and go as it pleases?

Would it be the wind otherwise?

One Essential Heart

I KNOW NOW THAT THERE HAS never been a time in my life when I haven't loved you. And I've always known this, even though it's only recently that I've come to understand how this could possibly be so.

There is a Center to all things, whatever their nature.

I'm not speaking of a physical location, necessarily; but of that True Center in and of any creation which is its essential Core, its fundamental Cause. Even casual observation more than supports this premise.

When I look out upon my surroundings as I did early this morning, and I behold the tall evergreens set so firmly into the mountains; the always-singing, often quarreling, spring-time birds — I seem not so much to see these individual forms as I am given to feel their presence. And this presence is apprehended by my heart whose vision is more acute . . . for it sees there is only one Heart at the center of all it beholds.

This One, Essential Heart, includes my heart, which rather than feeling itself diminished by its newly found knowing, actually feels itself increased — because this newly found knowing reveals that the center of this One Heart is Love. Timeless, and Itself having no center, this Love is neither here nor there, now or then — but is found in any and all places where there is heart enough to perceive It as being the Center of itself.

To touch this Love is to have known love for all time since this love embraces all loves future and past. And so I know from this touch: I have always loved you.

And I will . . . Always.

Come, and let me breathe you.
Let me draw you in and push you out,
Until you long to be drawn in once more.

Let me remind you of the Life I am
And of the Life that you may be.

Let my silent sighing move your soul to breathe me deep.
And if you'll remember my breath is yours,
You'll never forget your life is my air.

Come, let me breathe you myself and so
Gently will we be our breath breathing.

The Real Illusion

FIRST HE SAYS, "IT'S THE FULL-ness of life that's the illusion," because the Emptiness visits him so fully.

Then he says, "No, it's the emptiness of life that's the illusion," because the Fullness is upon him.

Back and forth, forth and back again, he swings between Fullness and Emptiness, Emptiness and Fullness . . . until one fine day . . . it dawns on him: The *real* illusion is the cup.

The Wedding

With this pain
I give thee Life
And do thee wed.

One Last Lesson:
Letting Love Lead You Home to Her
Some words of encouragement from the author

LOVE EXISTS. SHE IS NEVER not present although her life-giving presence is rarely perceived, much in the same way as we breathe in air moment to moment barely noticing the gift of life it sustains.

Nothing exists without Love. She is the secret Heart of all. These are not just words. They are an introduction to an Invitation created when Time began. To what are we invited? To *know* that we are already a measure of Love's Timeless Life . . . if we will only agree to learn the lessons she has prepared for us, beginning with this:

Love knows whom *She* will, and none may come to know her treasures without Her decision to divulge them. Yet, though Love may not be coerced to bestow her Grace upon a person — regardless of even the most dedicated efforts — She does have one secret faintness: Love longs to be loved, so She loves to be courted. And it is because of this most unique feature that the universe itself (that She alone unifies) literally lines up for anyone who will embrace it for Her sake, gently guiding this same person to the realm of Her timeless Life.

Now in everyone is sown — into the center of his or her soul — *some* love. Of this we may be certain, even though many people today seem counter-testimony to this Truth. Nevertheless, as obscured as Love's presence may be in someone we know or — and more to the point — as dim as She may shine within us from time to time — Love *is* there.

Love is that latent interior "hunger" we have *to know* whatever it is that we long to know. Love understands that whatever we will agree to *draw near to* ensures — given time — that we will come *to know* it; and then, transformed by Her magic through a marriage of a sort, we become *as one* with what was once unknown to us.

Don't think this too strange an idea. The hidden Principle of Love is that only through Her do we find in the object of our affection something of *ourselves:* that proverbial missing piece of the perennially empty heart.

The beauty of Love is that She is *already* within everything; which means that there is nothing that we are drawn to know by Love's invitation that won't grant us *for our journey itself* the gift of a greater relationship with Love. Now here is what these last few ideas have been leading up to:

If we want to receive love we have to give it. What this means is that we must journey to Her before She will consent to be known. *This* is the courtship Love requires of those who long to possess Her. Of course it's mysterious, but who doesn't love a mystery!

Now, in far more practical terms, here are some ideas how to begin this journey of the Heart:

First, give your love to *something. Do* something with your love. Find something *you* love and then set out to make it your own. Never mind if you don't have any one love for any one thing in this life. Forget the whole idea of love for the moment and ask yourself: "To what am I drawn? What is it that interests me?"

Whatever impressions you may feel from this sincere inquiry are the invisible magnetic impulses of a secret Heart, a pulse of Love that has been buried in you beneath layers — perhaps lifetimes — of misdirection. That is why you must take the next few instructions to heart.

Never mind if you are attracted to something but feel unable to start because you are afraid of failing in your quest. Be assured of this: Whatever it may be that you are drawn *to know* — whether it is to learn a new skill, grow a flower garden, develop an artistic skill, to help others, design clothes or cars, or set out towards a deeper interior life whose center is Love Herself — I tell you the only thing that matters is that you just start!

You can't know this yet, but it is Love that calls you to Her side for whatever is your eventual choosing, and it is Love within you that feels this drawing. So do you know what this means? Just consider: Love will not, *cannot* fail Herself. It is more likely the sun would fall from the sky than for Love not to begin to shine through your nascent efforts. Your first reward will be to feel the warmth of knowing you are nearing the beginning of a whole New Life.

Forget what others may think of you for your new aim to do your heart's desire. Disregard those whose reality is a rut! Misery wants company. Do Love's bidding instead. Persist with your working wish and Love will grant you the company of Herself. And as you gradually draw nearer to Her side you will know that nothing anyone thinks towards you could possibly add one cubit to your stature.

Brush aside any concerns you have (for whatever the reasons) of being unable to make a "big" beginning. *Just start where you are and with what you have* — even if this means taking a step so small that not one person on earth notices you have just left one world and entered another. Any beginning that you will make for the sake of answering the call of your heart is the same as a beginning whose happy ending *already resides right within that same initial action.*

Don't be the least concerned if you can't seem to find the time — or the energy — to get going because of life's seemingly endless "duties" to family or friends. Drop these punishing (and false) ideas. Listen instead to this promise that Love makes to anyone willing to draw near enough to hear Her whisper Her secret:

Do what you must to *make time* and you will see that *the energy you need to succeed* will be *given to you.*

Love lends her force to the entire universe, so don't you think that if you were to ask rightly for a bit of it — for Her sake — that She would give you the measure you need? Of course She will! All you need do is just make *some* time, *give* some moments to your intended journey. Even if all you can muster to get started with is two minutes a day, just place your attention on what you want to love, and it will love you back by giving you a bit of itself.

Persist with this new Work until you see — which you will

if only you will stay the course — that the love you thought you had chosen was really Love choosing you. And when at last you realize that it has always been this way, then, *for you*, it will always be so . . . until the end of time.

How may you be assured that all of this is True?

It is Love that tells you so.

Never the End

About the Author

GUY FINLEY is the acclaimed author of more than 24 books and audio albums on the subject of self-realization, and over the last 20 years has recorded over 1,000 separately entitled seminars presented to students all over the world. His most popular books, several of which have become international bestsellers are published in 15 languages. His work is widely endorsed by doctors, professionals, and religious leaders of all denominations. In the last twenty years, Guy has appeared on over 400 national and local radio and TV programs, including Coast to Coast, Sally Jesse Raphael, Entertainment Tonight, Michael Jackson, the Wisdom Channel, and many more.

TO WRITE TO THE AUTHOR

Guy Finley lives and teaches in southern Oregon. If you would like to write to the author about his book, receive information about his ongoing classes, or request a catalogue of his works (along with a free helpful study guide), send a self-addressed, stamped envelope to:

Guy Finley
Life of Learning Foundation
P.O. Box 10-A
459 Galice Rd
Merlin, OR 97532
Office: 541.476.1200   Fax 541.472.0822

A FREE GIFT FOR YOU

For a complete list of over 100 life-healing works by Guy Finley, visit his award-winning, multimedia website at **www.guyfinley.com**. Browse through all of the free resource materials; read or listen to excerpts from selected books and tapes. Request a free poster filled with helpful guidance and join the Foundation's free **"Key Lesson"** Club. Each week you'll receive an encouraging inner-life insight delivered right to your desktop via e-mail.

ABOUT LIFE OF LEARNING FOUNDATION

Life of Learning is a nonprofit organization founded by author Guy Finley in 1992. Its foremost purpose is to help individuals realize their true relationship with Life through higher self-studies. The Foundation is operated and run solely by volunteers. Everyone is welcome.

Guy Finley speaks four times each week at the Foundation to the men and women who gather there to learn more about self realization. Everyone is invited to come and share in the powerful transformational atmosphere that permeates each insight-filled talk. Each meeting awakens new energies, deepens intuitive powers, heals past hurts, and delivers welcome relief.

Life of Learning rests in the heart of southern Oregon's most beautiful country upon fourteen acres of old growth Sugar Pine. Visitors enjoy the beautiful flower gardens, organic foods, and walking trails with special places for meditation along the way. Twice a year the Foundation hosts special retreats for out-of-state students during the third week of December and June. The Talks in the Pines are an annual favorite.

Whether you enjoy its wild rivers, scenic lakes, old growth forests, mountain hiking, or strolling along the rugged Pacific Coast, when you visit Life of Learning you're only minutes away from Nature at her best. Life of Learning is located in the community of Merlin, Oregon. Just 7 miles away, is the city of Grants Pass. Visit **www.guyfinley.com** and request a visitor's pamphlet for a list of local accommodations.